For Greatness &
Freedom I Came
Faust or Fast?

Bill F. Ndi

Langaa Research & Publishing CIG
Mankon, Bamenda

Publisher

Langaa RPCIG
Langaa Research & Publishing Common Initiative Group
P.O. Box 902 Mankon
Bamenda
North West Region
Cameroon
Langaagrp@gmail.com
www.langaa-rpcig.net

Distributed in and outside N. America by African Books Collective
orders@africanbookscollective.com
www.africanbookscollective.com

ISBN-10: 9956-551-18-x

ISBN-13: 978-9956-551-18-7

© Bill F. Ndi 2020

Praise for this Poem

In this volume, Bill F. Ndi is a poet aware of and concerned about the current socio-political psychosis thriving around him, blemishing, choking, and drowning a once-upon-a time beacon turned into a madhouse. Ndi's frustrations are felt in his satiric wit, his luminous erudition savored in the beauty of his style which regurgitates past events and with the present tide, weaves them into an admonishing whole inspired by a disturbing premonition about the blind leading the blind in an otherwise near idyllic abode.

Emmanuel Fru Doh, PhD.
Department of English Century College Minnesota, MN USA

Strikingly powerful; this one sentence book length poem opens human conscience to the ways in which politics and riches destroy people and how humans struggle with being defined by the stigma of past centuries. Gripping and compelling from start to finish.

Maimo Mary Mah,
Development Communication Specialist/Consultant.

The poem cuts through societal malfeasance and corruption and delivers an acerbic, yet insightful attack on all that is wrong in the world. The poem throws hot snake oil and venom on evil spilling blood under the guise of religious consumption and browbeating legislators who can't remember their function. The poem is a barbecue feast of sacred cows and reminds of the human decency that was once a staple in a world striving for sanity.

Benjamin Hart Fishkin,
Associate Professor of English, Tuskegee University,
AL USA

For Greatness and Freedom I Came.
Faust or Fast?

Nightly news comes up
At six o'clock and rock
The waves with stale tale
Of another black man choked
Held out of breath
As I hold my breath tomorrow
Will bring news of the murderer
Committed his fear for his life
Pushed him to take
Away life from the innocent
Whose crime is always his skin
Endowed by nature at no cost
But used to make and generate
The devil's flyer for a rat race
In which we hear rumors
Of the stock market flying
Sky high before hitting
The bottomless pit
Dragged down by a moron
Hailed by avenge-elites
Screaming for black blood
To be drowned first with claims
He was of another clime and time
Not their hereness and nowness
Wrapped with the devil's bills
Cut from tax payers
And hailed businessman extraordinaire
And I wonder what Exupéry's
Would do with the stars

He claims his and cannot fathom
Maybe his extraordinariness
His watching hundreds of thousands
Drop like flies to an unseen
Messenger send to humble
The haughty and the bawdy
Chest thumping the world is theirs
When to it they are but passers-by
Whose empire would embrace insipidity
When they are boxed and entombed
For ants on which they trampled
To feast and make merry
In the underworld of colonies
With kings and queens
The nations work for and feed fat
While they care not for news reel fake, real,
Or cooked or burnt
Yet, our moron calls all he favors
Not fake as they prick where it hurts
Or so does to dog whistle
To a base none need debase
For that's their throne and crown
Found in the dustbin of history
My forebears forfeited
For their divisiveness
And trends pithing the haves and the have nots
The plebes and the royal clowns
Red and blue blood
Nonsense given weight to more than Marley's
The color of a man's eye
Whose only significance is far flung
From the putrefied piece of human flesh

Unable to recall its cowardly cry
For individuality and greatness
Fleeting and lulling he has dominion
Over a world in which he's sent
To sojourn for a stint he mistakes
For eternity which is hereafter
For those though not color blind
See the beauty of a tableau
The various flowers in nature
Created for the comfort of eyes
Filter rainbow colors through their prism
In which America the beautiful
Reads prison to incarcerate
Black bodies for theirs are the scum of the earth
Decried by Fanon from the first
World they delight to call the third
From their fourth world oval desk
By which a vulture with the brain of amoeba
Tweets inanities
Applauded by a deplorable bunch
In hope might has always been right
Knowing not might trite
In the grand scheme of things to come
Foe there is no race that the winner
Was the starter but always the finisher
Lifted the trophy across the finish line
Wherefrom a look behind would never
Be in anger nor would it need
Chicken soup with barley
Nor trumpet the western world for show-boys
Who think not slaves
Could themselves pull up

From their bootstraps,
Fight, die, and win independence
For the nation that enslaved them for centuries,
Legislate in both houses
In the early days,
Advise presidents and win world wars too,
Change the course of music over five times
Before going to sit in the house by slave ancestors built
The rest whitewashed as theirs
For everything by blacks built
Must to naught be brought
For the last challenge stabs
At the very heart of a myth
And lie mythomaniacs
Cart and disseminate
Turning sun in broad daylight
Moon and night day
The moron a sage
And conman savior
Heralded God given
From the pit of we know what
That leaves the ghostly heart kin up in arms
To defend a stronghold
In a mountain cave
With expectations set high
And great above the sky
In vain attempt to avoid mountain climbing
Relegated to chimney sweepers
And to cotton pickers
Whose hirsute times mold
Hell hard ones to make sense
Of and pride themselves

With prejudice without sensibility
Flying the individual flag
Of a dog in a world of dog eat dog
With this dog eating and refusing
To be eaten as starvation the uncanny weapon
Will compel and make Satan's
Thinking of man living by bread
Alone unhampered though put to shame
For at the origin of sight is unseen
For blazing light blinds
And the proverbial grass far from greener
On the other side
In which the rat race yields
And epidemic of opioid
Leaving behind my kind
Thought to feel no pain
They endured from the house
Of Potiphar and in their plantations
That could only constrain the body
Leaving the soul free to roam
The heavens where bliss abounds
With one love for us to get together
And feel alright away from America
Where breath seizing ruinous robbers
Murder Peel's Bobbies in the name
Of keeping the peace
They uphold by locking others
Out of the garden these others cultivate
To sparkle their face with play of firelight
Langston Hughes uses to take America
Back to the bedrock of civilization
Along rivers whereby black wail

Give me liberty or give me death
And herein delight is in giving death
With the newest of trends
Being to compel parents
To have children layover at school
Before making it home to the grave
As this injunction will serve the interest
Of the insane willing to sit
In the whitewashed house
Just because a spec of the minority
Roamed the halls and sat at tables
Therein to brew the venom
That led the clown they crowned
To saying he'd pay for their crime
As this would herald him to prime time
Along with his cohorts of pro-lifers
Who care more for their dogs
Than fellow humans nothing but the dose
Of melanin in their hide
The unknown key
To human essence and the destruction of which
Shall turn America on her head
For her to pass out that which comes out
From behind to so do through the mouth
As often happens to he who the pillar
Stone rejects and casts away
In the deep of the sea
With little to no knowledge
He'd have to dive and drown in searching
Such lost philosophical stone
Draped in wisdom infinite
That all attempts to out-wisdom

End in a hole the color of which
Is of the forgiving reject
Letting go the ignorance all humans
One way or another
Dead or alive
Had been rejects ejected
And thrown in a cavernous
Harbor whose grotto man
Should not measure
For each attempt ends
When he counts six feet
At night with a hoot from the owl
And not the bald eagle herein flown
In utter pride and arrogance
As if this fowl were manmade
With his thought life on earth
A hallmark forever of muscle flexing
Blind to concrete breaking
Mushroom with no muscles
They dream to squash with
Fabrications ours has no history
To hold our hands across the bridge
Where still with vain attempt
They'd endeavor to bury a mold
When from clay the first man
Was baked brown dust to which he'd
Someday
Return to make peace
Some scorn out of reach for AA
And if you wish Mandel's
As if there's a crime to pay back debt
Promised to be an acre and a mule

Later traded for Jim with his crow
Dressed in black with a white noose
For neck collar to take back
That which has not been taken
Centuries back to the years
One half dominion had
Over the other and chattelizing
Him three fifth person
Thus a house divided between itself
With invite to China and Russia
To venture their vultures
In the streets of the district
With such check as none would have
Ever dreamt to take to any
With any hopes to be cashed
Or deposited for future
Bite from burped up wisdom
Running to embrace negation
Denying even ocular damages
Inflicted on the environment
As much as that against
Fellow man for only one nation
Must stand to bully and the bully
They've sat on the throne
To shove hate down the throats
Fox pooh fixed and wrapped
With gilded rants against liberals
Wanting freedom purported
Rebellion against the Almighty
Whose decree is for man to be free
Here on earth and in the here after
Where our choice will be the dictate

8

Of life lived by the books and not
By spilling blood under the guise
Of fighting God's battles
When he never assigned you to
For He has the dominion America
Would appropriate for herself
With dog whistle to blood mongers
Mongering black blood as they
Do black gold
For which wars in the name of freedom's
Protection are waged but when exposed
To God's unseen hand
Weaknesses fly full mast
And the world cast a laughing glance
At the naked emperor with putrid
Bowel content he takes for cake
Just because he'd had a piece of cake
He deems the most delicious ever
With none asking to whom
It tastes so nor whose judgment
Such is for his wit is prefixed
With nit so is his intelligence
And oxymoron
Broadening red square smiles
To the vexation of the fabric
Only a buffoon would want torn
As would a wanton boy a fly
He ignores plays a role in renewing
And recycling one time composition
Churn in the compost
Used to fertilize and grow little bowls of health
Desirable to ward off the toxic stench

You by the second emit
Taking for perfume
Bombarding senses to bid the devil
To heed William Shakespeare
And quote the bible with claims
And tall tales
The all forgiving God has listened
To his prayers and has readmitted
His arch-rival into heaven
And has thus relocated heaven
To this part of the world
Wherein good old Quakers
For witches were hunted
For embracing the light from
Within and the crime of chanting
A Christ in all mankind
Though master was equal
Amongst peers and disciples
Without exception which could not sit
Well in the land of exceptionalism
That shield capitalism
Making use of individuals
For capital making machine
Whose humanness must be sat on
And by inhumanity taken for a ride
And when questioned for having
A hand in the cookie jar
Just when all eyes wandered away
Ejaculates insults for daring
The crocodile in baby gator swamp
He came to drain clad in his suit
So none would reckon him swamp dweller

Whose way to the swamp he must con
In power tricks wherein admirers
Delight in lies to herald such
Champion godsend messiah
None needs to judge for the good books
Prohibit and not even when shy of four
Years he unpacks eighteen thousand
Dishonest or deceptive claims
In eleven seventy days
During which he'd swayed
With a candy a nation he rapes
For it is convenient to point the finger
At others for the crime
They are not guilty
But must the bane carry
For the Big Bully on Campground
At whose sight one cannot help
But wonder what substance he's high on
To browbeat his house
And have his senate quake
Wherein graham pees his pants
And tears in hope history
Be soft on him for selling
His soul in a Faustian bargain
He heralded on a campaign stage
To denounce the con in chief
To be his spiritual guide
With him going on his knees
Each time the bully farts
For him to sniff and praise
How sweet the smell out-smells
The roses bushmen smell

Before coming out to civilization
Wherein they dare to claim manly
Fullness in the land of the braves
Whose foolhardiness is in oppressing
And striking the strings of pain
To which blackness is insensitive
And such clouded thought and thinking
Black eyes alone can see
In white dark night
Shielding white cowards to torch
Crosses with fire with which forebears
Kept and keep humanity from extinction
Unlike the braves pushing for a crime
Syndicate within which the boss
Sits on the shoulders of his lackeys
And drinks form the fount of enslavement
Defended by delusional enraged knaves
Reveling in tyrannizing and terrorizing
With the preservation of shame
And relics of the beast in man
Who from the shackles of the walls of Jericho
Fled into a new world
Growing the dreams of building walls
To keep children of the universe
As if their labors coming out of the forest
Climbing hills and mountains
And struggling for breath through
The middle passage to sweating
In their plantation to build their economic
Foundation with white gold
Picked by black hands reduced to less
Than the desirable images of God's own

Image he makes His pride far from
Man's heralded pride steeped in debauchery
That spared not Sodom nor Gomorrah
Nor any other civilization taking
Icarus for a myth to wander
Close to such burning sun flame
And the phoenix their reality
To be reborn from their own ashes
Which I know not ashes from hell
To fertilize any other land than a heath
For the glorification of man
Poor poor miserable man
Plodding down the paved boulevard
To the blazing furnace
In which they would they pushed my kind
To deprive them of a history
To deprive them of a language
To deprive them of an education
To deprive them of a religion
To deprive them of a memory
To deprive them of their humanity
To deprive them of their right to live
To deprive them of their pursuit of happiness and Liberty
To deprive them of a culture
To deprive them of the right to breathe free air
The goal of which is to bewitch
Souls Mother Nature would flourish
Unhindered and not by those willing
To deal and steal God's supremacy
To inflict pain
To give grief
To grow sorrow

To chain bodies
To distort facts
To still breathing
To inject sickness
To stifle growth
To cut the tongue
To stab the eyes
To cultivate ignorance
To highjack their thoughts
To pit one against another
To feed them shit
For the foes dire desire
To play God when all they are
Are frightened chicks
Scared to death divine wrath
Dwindles the population
Having buried the love for neighbors
Replete in their Sunday sermons
Which they joy to hear on Sunday
To turn coat and spend the week
Aspiring to harvest greatness by slighting
Slaughtering and burying others'
Greatness
Peace
Love
Freedom
Passion
Vision
Voices
Dreams
Drive
Happiness

Forgiveness
Knowledge
Spirit
Faith
Nobility
Dignity
Integrity
Understanding
Kindness
Needs
Memory
Triumph
Birth right
Though they came not here to be oppressed
Nor was desperation their goad
Than was the opportunity
To advance humanity
With her door for growth shut here
Torturing the brains to make sense
Of the world around
One where the hands of time
At work to align the cosmos
Is twisted in effort to stop
Them from work and give
Salivation through a wall to exclude
Just in time for Mother Nature to hurtle
In and tell who has might and dominion
Over man and his demonic master and evil thought
Whose art exhibit brings to the fore
Cracks and oiling lava in readiness
To spill and manure the strong new breed
Green red yellow black and white

Won't give way to the blues
Whose rhythm won't torture
Pink Floyd-y souls with jazzy trumpet
Sounds calling souls to repent
And get ready for the kingdom
In spite of appalling enslavement
Our foundation for spiritual growth
As we search for the Promised Land
Far away from the sunset hemisphere
That failed to produce a magi
To spot and understand a star born
Thereabouts or that dropped seeds
From sold human beast of burden
Would grow to gravitate around their white
Mansion spun from Jenner's wheel
Just as he begins to understand
Why his forebears' sale was allowed
In the first place which has been to show
Him the up and downhill road to wisdom
Divine and infinite
Flowing down the rivers besides
Which they have nursed humanity
To the monstrosity
Standing on the way of human
Revolution with pride of monopoly
To a rebellion that parachuted them here
Now obliterating the first blood drop
In that quest for freedom was black
As the only good with black
Associated is gold
White or black
The one by hand picked

The other under his feet drilled
And channeled with smiles
To the market for the Green backs
Which flashed Puerto Rico in the news
One weekend with revelation
This soul of America pushed to the edge
Of being sold for an environmental disaster
Visiting her was the greatest crime no
Piece of land should ever suffer
To welcome from nature reacting
To man's greed turning natural green
Into those that allow buying and selling
Of bombshells for the content
Of the earth's bowel nature buried
To rid the planet of the undesirable
Element
Man drills as if to unearth buried
Human bowel content
Before scuttling away to hide
His nose under a piece of hide
Peeled off the dark kin's skin
To appropriate the lynching
And skinning to match with a trite none could
Dream and make of a race
You forced the human race
Into as the starter with no knowledge
Races aren't for starters but finishers
For as true beginners to finish strong
Painful and slow the pace could be
But stout and strong the resistance would be
In your face for yours as confrontation is
Not to reflect humility

But claims of one who never fault
Found in his dealings
And never for once saw need
To ask for pardon
Or much needed forgiveness
To open the door to peaceful
Co-existence with harmonious melody
To spin the world on its axis
To complete the revolution with no haste
In the tradition of refinement
Calling for hardship and roughness
To smoothen the rough edges
And bring to mind
The conditions of gold or diamond
Long before we see their glitter
Which are nothing near glorious
And telling those who themselves glorify
Over others they ignore
The irritant sands on seashells
Do smoothen and sheen the shells
As heat the gold
And cold the diamond
Whose sparkles razzle and dazzle
Before we learn the next lie
From a bird's tweet pushed
By tiny birdy fingers
That golfs with no competitor
To be a champion raised
In Moscow and put in
And hailed by accomplices as a hoax
Which hoax stands for everything
We see dragging down the giant

Including the airborne general
Who in his own right brought
Millions to their knees
And put to sleep hundreds of thousands
Because the know-it-all head man
Won't agree with specialists
Except they are part of the syndicate
Singing his song for the crumbs
Of his biscuits wrapped in commutation
And handed out as communion
From the hands of the highest
Priest of meanness his most excellent thief
Who has invented a new art form in town
Painting truth and dressing her with all
New alternate reality
For a country wherein movies
Pass for real life
And real life for filth
That needs not dirty New York's fifth
Avenue on which stands the mast
Of blood dough
Twisting the arms of states
To dump down the vigor
With which to stand against sporty
Corvette appropriating nineteen
And showing the highest office
In the land
Desecrated with the nation's
Highest honor handed
Over to a fascist rabble rouser
As the vacant oval office
And shadow grand wizard

To the clan and son of a Klansman
Hands over the toy confounding
Far right wing with Right
Which he knows not to be true
For right is right
Anywhere anytime
In rainfall in sunshine
And in any clime and time
And cannot be blown away
By wind nor eroded by weathering
And little less by constant hammering
Of lies about anything and everything
That does not honor the executive disgrace
Ignoring the presence of "I" and "H"
In Triumph for which he takes himself
Just because he's never heard
Of Percy Bysshe Shelley
And his king of kings
Whose colossal wreck
Overwhelmed and antique traveler
From the distant land of bad
Ombres crossing borders with diseases
And drugs the like of ill-wind
Bringing no one good
But to the monster who'd
On them prey and have them
To him bow claiming he's master
Yes of mischief being a thief in chief
With clayey feet
And a fiery pit of hell mind
Throwing punches far below the belt
And at the umpire for punks

Want a revolution to take far to the right
And happening before the eyes of do
Nothing good Christians
Whose ears never got wind
Of guilt and hope,
Exile in the Fatherland
Of old pastor Niemöller who came
By revelation that one's God given voice
Is both instrument of praise
And glorification as well
As that for the defense of Zion's
Prisoner in Babylon
Where inaction
Writes a page in history
Of a nation none would want
To turn to in the future
For the embrace of that inconsistent
Form of government to civil society
John Locke asked be made
Garbage for the dustbin of history
For human society to be great
And here we come to revisit
Locke's society to MAGA
With embraces of dictacracies around the world
And forfeiture of freedom flag
Flying at half mast
While that of shame goes full mast
With the justification of a love
Affair with and for NASCAR
To shield Freedom of speech
Which warrants rejoinders such
As whites are also killed

In response to a question
On the disproportionate use of force
And police brutality against the pigmented
Whose demise seem not to wake
The slightest sense of empathy
To the least racist president the world
Has ever known
And whose political outing
Underlined his pre-revolutionary thinking
Of blacks not being whole
And consequently not citizens
To ground his challenge
Of a pigmented being part and parcel
Of this here now country
To whom he must slam all the vices
The world has ever known
As his dog whistle to good people
At work to muddy the waters
In Charlottesville
And send Heather Heyer home to rest
And then trounce the union with blues
In their macabre farcical circus show
In which the master clown
Behind a red nose and a grin
Hides base psychopathy to steal
Away the hue of man to make man
And not hue with man
For their want in emotion
They've carved out of Dickens'
Hard Times' stock of Bounderby and Bitzer
Whose reading of life is but a bargain
Across the counter with gain

As its apex and apogee
And stone coldness the walls
Within which they dwell
To obliterate the past
And Renaissance's Copernicus
For whose statement and stance
Levy a heavy price on Galileo
For centuries pointing that which
Was the center of the universe
And now the young Copernicus
Commits another crime
Going on his knee
To drop the mask and show the nation
Her central concern
Only to be monetized as treason
To conceal that of mysterious
Submission and mutism
In the face of charges against bounties
On the boys in green
By the enemy king maker
Turned kingfisher
After the big fish this here nation has become
With the smallest head making for ease to swallow
Before hacking her endeavor to bring to a halt
A virus invisible to the eyes
And the clown in chief dares not
For he is beholden to the crime boss
Of the red gang resident at red square
Would love the big league
To be part of his circus of clowns
Amongst whom the clown
In chief would he his place take

Reckoning not abandonment in the cold
Brought him to his knees
And would so do to bring down
His new supersonic Tupolev
With whose speed Children
Are from parents snatched
And in pigsty dumped
In the name of my country over all
Others thus sending shock waves
Through the doctrine of universality
Of the declaration that once calmed the turbulent
Sea of racial discrimination
Now crucified to hug the alt right
That flipside of alright
From the time he walked down
The monstrosity on Fifth Avenue
With outlandish claims
That made jerks cheer and others laugh
He'd never shoot and kill as he claimed
And get away with murder
And he lived to prove the KGB
Handbook one to keep CIA
And FBI sleepless for years unend
With barr barring the way to justice
Preventing the law from throwing
Behind bars jackal that would lie not to serve
Yet would heroes insult for their duty to fatherland
Deaden soul lackeys and knaves
Compounded with congressional
Holdup
All dancing to the wind of betrayal
To please the straight-face lying president

Depleting pluralism
To champion
Brutalization
Ghettoization
Gentrification
Polarization
Fragmentation
Separation
Discrimination
Dehumanization
De-Americanization
De-Westernization
And Russianization
All to take a new moniker
Of America first
At the expense of allies
Left awondering if the word trust
Ever a sense made
Seeing Soviet style assault
Of Portland by anonymous unidentified
Feds as was in DC a while back
Where streets were smoked clean of humans
For a clown to stand up
For a photo opportunity
Holding the bible upside-down
With chants of law and order
When children have eyes to read
Lawlessness and chaos
As number forty five
Speaks to highlight lies
For every time he speaks he lies
And so lies he every time he speaks

And criminalizes innocence
Even when one of such
Twenty eight Times pleads
For breath that would bring forth change
And when the quest for change
Comes he greets the quest
With the destruction of suburbs
Laying the foundation
For legalization of Criminalization
With dreams we'd stream to the morgue
Chanting funeral song
We refuse to sing the dirge
For ours shall and must remain
A song of hope that'd break
The yoke around our necks
And when we lament it would be
With joy of Paul and Silas
Stinging worse than a bee
And bringing down prison walls
Many before us have been
Fighting to bring down
The likes of a good old friend
John Lewis gone to be
With Brother Elijah Cummings
After a good fight
Heeding a call come from glory
After six plus decades
In a struggle he inherited from King
Who inherited from forebears
Who inherited from the first man
Distracted then as we are today
By a green sneaky snake in the green

Grass of the lawn spawning seeds
Of hate blind war sheep ass
Take for a march into history
While on the windward side
Of the mountain with us on the leeward
Letting down poll numbers
In a free fall to slap him to wake up
From his stance and claim of perfection
Before heaping the blames on others
And claim mask wearing an act of patriotism
For as he says none but he takes responsibilities
Which he would he did shifting stance
For ratings not for human life
Swept away by fear of the ballot coffin
That pushed humpty-dumpty
To climb the fence with corona
Daily briefing from whence with kinsmen
He'd fall with his fleet of lies
For which he is called out
And he flies his flag of ignorance
With fix news where not a hiss
Comes to quest the bounty
On our boys' head by his demon master
Dwelling in red and wanting the world
All drenched in red of black blood
An echo intoning music to the ears of that bigot
Whose twisted mind would history twist
As Shakespeare holds of the devil
Quoting the bible to suit his intentions
Just as does our forked tongue
Playboy who delights in grabbing
The essence of human origin

With impunity and mannish foolishness
Raising his shoulders above his head
To bully poodle Mitch to cower
As he squats when any mentions
red followed by square
put follow by in
rush followed by shear
to sharpen his wit to defend
spy master string puller
with Pavlovian drool to see us fall
When in flight the bald
Eagle gains altitude
To remind him hawks
Would never bathe in this highness
Nor fly in the same clouds
As ours donning their silver lining
Which warrant our stars to shine bright
And magnet envy from the incarnate
Dreaming of beating a record
Nikita Khrushchev
Dreamt he would hold in his grave
Only to be heart broken by moon landing
Before giving up his ghost
To where it belonged
Having renounced the very origin
Of his own essence
And daring to play the creator
From a playbook by which our house's
Occupant seems to play
With effrontery he has never
Had a need to seek forgiveness
For he was the best student but we'd never

Know what his transcripts hold
Nor would any ever be told
This callous stone coldness
The cream of outrageousness
Talking of world wars in terms
That snap mouths open
To wondering if the moron
Fathoms an oxymoron
To wear his batch of career
Assassin to those who dare
To speak truth to power
As he in vain attempt to vie
Against nations located light
Years from his get-worse-to-better
Stead with no nous from stopping
It from getting worse
Which is the hallmark of leaders
With ripe balls
And not those with deflated balls
Like our lashing out vengeful king
Who in a minute tells us of patriotism
And the next we see him with his coat
Turned to reflect his outburst of verbiage
He delights in pushing down the throats
Of the nation's institutions he's selling
And dragging down the drain leading
To the swamp he swore he'd drain
While the fringe elements reveled
Knowing he was swearing all in vain
Only to promote their odium
Agenda with her opium
Toxic hand used to shred apiece

That which he was sworn in to protect
Yet he is always providing evidence
To the contrary to create
A useful political spectacle
Against the defense of the constitution
Dragged down to the pits of hell
By taking his dictatorial campaign message
To the height of Putin-like
Turning and tipping point
To make a moron a strong man
And the innocent the bogeyman
For taking down the weight
His neck can no longer take
When abhorrence is pushed
To the apogee unconcerned
With Human Live constantly buried
In the sewer of crime and violence
Which have no place where the edifice
Of our constitution stands strong
And keep the scale balanced
Tipping it not to suit the whims and caprices
Of a flat foot draft dodger
And plagiarist who copies
And makes the originator squirm
In the grave as does Millhouse
This day wondering where he'd kept
His grey matter to becoming the Quaker
Disgrace kept in in cold wet room
In which belongs the cohort of treasonous
Felons parading before cameras
And hailing a crook a savior
And one who happens to be born

On a bad hair day
And has since his first day
Kept evil raging and slouching
Towards autocracy with them
Living and breathing gangsterism
And always invoking God to tell lies
Lying about anything and everything
Mindless the soul of this nation
Stands on foundation Fox would
Yea be yea nay be nay
Far from the embrace
Of this retaliatory machinery
Followed by those who refuse
To learn to recognize the lies
Satan warps in toxic misogyny
Against which soldiers and apostles
Of Truth and the rule of law
Would till the last man standing fight
To rid America of the trust killer
Whose every breath sows seeds of doubts
Whose every breath sows seeds of discord
In those willing to set alight
The house of freedom under
The guise they have the mandate
To put up God's fight for Him
Because liberals demand freedom
Which is equipollent to Satan's
Rebellion and exemplification of weakness
Which gives dictatorships around the world
Solace and a handful of kakistocrats
A reflection of the dark side of us
As if to point at the limits

Of freedom infinite as an illusion
In a world peopled by humans
Whose dire thirst for oligarchy
Would bring to question In God's Name
Whether there are lessons to learn
From dictators who with both sides of their mouths
Speak to laud evil and to lure the desirous
In want and need
For whom material wealth
Marks not opulence but recompense
From God for hard work
Which thinking ought to make the enslaved
Black man the wealthiest
Not within which world institutions
Are eroded to slowly refurbish
The black blight and plight
Against which generations have fought
And died to breathe a bit of air
They do everything to cut from him
Since a free black man though kind
Is unsettling in the oppressors' mind
Which knows no other way
To trap flies other than with a bucket
Of pus whereas black and brown
Would with a drop of honey
Honey sweet honey not money
That kills consciences
And enslaves man to taking his kin for a foe
Scapegoating immigrants
For they dare to dream
To be part of a dream dreamt
Which sparked the flames of jealousy

And today warranting dreamers be sacrificed
For rotten eggs willing to turn
A viral health risk into one
Of street gun violence
That flashes greenlight to oppress
And chip away checks and balances
Before carving rubber stamps
That would leave the nation
With desert sand in the eyes
Finding favor on the bench
With ears stuck out to gulp
Instruction and be fed ruling
To let bigotry be comfortable
Besides the arbiter and player
Who would neither pull the leash
Nor red card the fed leech
Who might be a friend from Russia
With no identification nor insignia
And also one who would have loved
To be the first man
'Coz he would have asked to be
Alone in the garden
So he would have the world to himself
As if the multiple colors of a tableau
Were the Artist's greatest mistake
To give privileged white boy
The chords with which to rant about
Foreign nationals out-earning whites
And the nuisance is not their foreignness
But their non-whiteness
Heckling mad bill who claims no knowledge
Of what it is to be white and privileged

Nor what it is to be a harasser
Nor why he settles and settles harassment claims
Made by women whose only desire
Is to lie with and about him
Framing it a culture of sexual harassment
Of and to which Roger the Sick succumbed
Before handing the baton to the insane bill
Of right to lie garbed as a commentator
Who's now caught the perfect time
To cling onto a leech who sees humans
Not as coming from countries but from places
Claimed by their cast to replicate
Car exhaust pipes in humans
Ejecting all their ingestions
And polluting the environment
Which with all in and on it
Are majoritarian belongings
With which no color should dare mess
For it will immediately invoke the ghost
Of the dreaded opium war
Who broke into China
Stole a piece of her canton
She kept for a hundred and fifty years
With a condition the stolen duck
Would remain the chicken of which the thief
With all his might strove to make
And with failure to do so comes a push
For arms twisting with choruses
Of defense of national security and prosperity
Once shredded and tossed in the bin
Of Russian intervention
And the hoop of Chinese meddling

To maintain a buffoon whose dream is to bully
All and sundry into submission
Finding an alacritous ally in an AG
And a branch of the legislature
To ride willing horses to death
And dares any attempts to squeeze the truth
To arm him with the dictionary
Of insults from which he curls
Words to dub and clobber questers
Evil
Mean
Nasty
Crooked
Silly
Stupid
Fake news agent and woe betides
Questioner were a woman
He'd grab a copy of two thousand
More insults
From which he'd prove
He has mastered the art of putting down
And can and will pull her down
With insults she never heard
And in a way she's never known
Not even when it was fashionable
To deem her kind without a soul
And a vessel weaker than weak
Because of his narrowness
To take questions his brain power
Cannot stand the nuclear bomb effect
Coming from such weak vessels
One of whom labored to push

Him out into this weird wide world
Wherein those who reckon God
Into the same world chose to come
Through the vessel man's wisdom
Deemed weaker would without condition
Ally with the bully and hail him godsend
And blessed with wealth, pride, and arrogance
Not forgetting lust for which he'd not repent
For repentance is for the weak
With whom he'd never be identified
To let the spotlight dim
And so must veer through the Carolinas
To ramble on plenty of discussion
With his Russian pal
While joggling the hot potato of COVID
He has spent time downplaying
And willing to sweep all under the rug
By sounding the drum of a great job
He and his have been doing very close
To shitocracies he was quick to name
With the colorful anatomical member
One would dare he blocks his for a day
And live for another day
Without finding faults with predecessors
From Washington to about the greatest
Who had been complaisant with Chinese rise
He and only he can fix
Alongside anything wrong with a nation
In which everything has been wrought
By and with moral bankruptcy
That spilled and is spilling black blood
 And challenges and warrants

A call to action to fight
For nothing but what is right
Wrongfully denied some members
Of the same household dispossessed
Of their humanity with lies buried
Under the French Revolutionary motto
Which drives a quest as to how
A foundation built upon
Subjugation
Could uphold and sustain
Liberty
And how capital raised
With blood sweat and tears
Would let thrive
Equality
And how the fears of the guilty
Gripped by the terror of reprisal
Could free the oppressor
To see the oppressed
Belonging to the same fraternity
Wherein the latter is willing to let go
Of his brothers' crime
Of yesteryears yet
Is reminded by the minute
He is only to be seen and not to be heard
Not even when he would his brothers
Reckon looking at the past
Straight in the face
And taking on her
The like of a torero to bring
To the dinner table entrées
Main dish and dessert

That would assuage the hunger
And thirst for ideals
That rattled Pilgrims' brains
For them to board the Mayflower
Dreaming they'd hold onto those dreams
We're reminded of by prophetic words
From the one and only John Lewis
Ringing true four hundred years after
With people willing to lead us
Into the darkness in which peace
Meant lynching
Scarification
Thing-ification
Reification
Commodification
Degradation
Dehumanization
Of the other while
Love meant renunciation
Of God's good creation
As embodying one people
Who now crave to finish the unfinished
Business that is the American Revolution
Fought by blacks and whites
Gay and straight
Christians Muslims Buddhists and pagans
Believers and non-believers
Whole persons
Three fifth person
Theist and agnostic
Africans
Indigenes

European
Asians
Scandinavians
All animated by the dream of togetherness
That is heralded to the pillory
For elimination
Exclusion
Segregation
Extinction
To kill and bury
Accountability
And his brother
Representation
Lying in state in the Rotunda
As the first of his kind
To be so laid
Confining the bigot a thousand feet away
At his base wherefrom he invokes
Pavlov's to his puppies
To flash ambers that the desire
For oneness is so not Arian
High-heartedness that doth bring
Bill to the house to perjure
In defense of heartlessness
With vain attempts to turn
Lies into veracities
And when caught with both hands
In the cookie jar
He'd haste to pick up
Pilate's crown and request
Water with which to wash his hands clean
For doing the right thing to preserve

More than two hundred and fifty thousand
Lives with blames of a predecessor
From whom none has heard in years
Though under him Ebola was kept at bay
And none carried the burden of lockdown
With whom the nation is wedded
In unholy matrimony
And must take the blows and smacks
And still be the loving battered wife
Humble and willing to take more jibes
From a hate of state
Self-styled wartime president
Akin to the mayor of Casterbridge
Selling wife and child to a stranger
As would this desperate miscreant
And object of pity
Standing strong to wedge war against our
Nation casting aspersions on our votes
And doing Russia's bidding
For he is in need of a father
And finds one in this devil
Willing to buy a nation over which to reign
And bury citizens' rights as he botched
Those of denizens
In the steppes of his birth
And in return he'd be garrisoned
With accusations against China
The most colorful diversion
That would have the crime syndicate
Turn a blind eye to bounties
Paid for our men and women to be haste
Out by the selling commander in chief

In readiness to give his devilish master
A smirk by breaking the rampart
In the German backyard
From whence checks chains and muzzles
Gave the evil empire bits and pieces
Of Dickensian hard times
With which to dress for almost
Four score years and leave
Knaves kidnapping to kill
Behind their robe and hood
In the closet out of which they come
Led by a loose cannon after Nike and Apple
Screaming like a madwoman after a wild
Bacchanalian spree with a demon lover
To ban products originating from slave labor
While defending shameless capitalism
And individualism at home
Where he wished tax cuts benefitted
Vultures and vampires imbibing
The blood of the nation with hate and fear
As well as trickle Down Reganomics
Erected by messiahs of personal ambition
And masons of infrastructures of oppression
To which the founding father of America of the future
Did in his days respond
With love and hope
As the dope
And incapacitator
To breakdown the machinery selecting
Lives that matter under the guise
Of all lives matter
When for earthly glory they kill

To claim world championship
At their best outwrestling the worst
In Pharaoh's Egypt
Where bad faith barr proves to be
The enemy from within granting
Legitimacy to this adage that
Conspiracies from without never triumph
And shedding light on this flashing beacon
On the American Revolutionary Reign of Terror
Imported from the Seventeen Eighty-Nine
French Revolution into the streets
Of American cities wherein
Peaceful protesters' pleas call the roll
Lafayette Square
Washington DC
Present
Portland Oregon
Present
Milwaukee Wisconsin
Present
Chicago Illinois
Present
All to test the grounds for a ruse
From a Red play book
That would make a con a king
Who like Milton's Satan
Finds support from a host
Of other fallen angels
Whose choice were by personal gain
Powered
With a twist they were once
Reigning angels

While this scam artist has all along been
A potentate to whom Raleigh
Would readily give a lie
For lies make him thrive
To label any fact against his phony
Fake news
And to pick gratuitous fights
With perceived enemies
Who are none but the figment
Of his invalid imagination
And this is rather an oxymoron for he has none
With which to measure the validity
Nor could one even take his secretary's
Who would cite security concerns
Over a first amendment promoting software
For he and his boss alone
Can with mud purify waters pellucid
Clean just as they alone would rather
Be king-gators in the swamp
Upon draining out the drainers
In whose gospel checks and balances scream
Stop to foreign aid and intervention
On our most cherished jewel
Adorning our democracy
Which Blackburn with a red carpet
Welcomes and would make sure they
Reside far faraway
From probing hungry eyes
Where they'd never be consumed
By the fervor for transparency
In a process the don would were opaque
As he wishes his swamp waters muddied

As he alone has eyes to see through the mud
With ears blocked not to hear
The voice and clamor of Democracy
Echoing from US cities' streets
Where area boys are deployed
'Coz with theft in his blood
These boys must make away with votes
To resolve personal
And above all legal
Problems
Flown on the mast of bank
And tax fraud
Flying in the face of the nation
Threatening to crash
Which threat grips his thoughts
And has his Tourette's syndrome kick
Him in the butt to screaming
Curses welcomed by Republican
Congressional hallelujah boys and girls
Led by ole Mitch who delights
His name echoes number fifty
So he'd call for the single word
Refrain to which they all screech out a hypothermic amen
In hope the latter crime the last
Of his pickaxe falling on the grave
He is digging them
For they scoff he'd learned
The infamous French expression
Après-moi le déluge
Which brings him great regret
And make him question how stupid Noah
Must have been to dirty the world

With different species whereas
He'd rather have survived alone
And kept the world to himself
And escaped any probe that doth rattle his brain
Though all know in place of gray
Matter his is dark matter
Through which trumpocrazy has let go
Two hundred and sixty thousand plus souls
To prove him a wartime leader
Who with trumpevangelists
Have found a panacea
For COVID in hydroxichloroquine
And the eighteen million worldwide
Infection is nothing but fake news
Ignoring trumpevagelical prescription
That has had more done for Black people
To the point of eradicating
And reducing the travails of my own John Lewis
To a child's play for with good reason
He'd ignored the nauseous stench
Of an inauguration even birds spited
Not to sell out that for which he'd fought
And for which he had laid his life
Against the virus of stupidity
Tellingly misleading
A well pronounced eulogy
Made the front pages of an angry
Column of fox and friends
All in total readiness to peddle
Masturbatory
Ululations for trumpnationalists
Holding up their clubs and guns

Waylaying the truth they've conjured
Into the forked tongue
Great deceiver mirrored
In their grand master
They take for the last bastion
Between the same master's master
And the Apocalypse
As they have their days numbered
Sheepishly leading themselves
Against the wanderings of Moses in the wilderness
In quest of milk and honey
Not for personal ambition but for the fulfillment
Of a divine assignment ...

Printed in the United States
By Bookmasters